A Celebration of the American Flag

WINTERS PUBLISHING

winterspublishing.com

DAIN TAYLOR

A Celebration of the American Flag

Published by:
Winters Publishing
P.O. Box 501
Greensburg, IN 47240
812-663-4948
winterspublishing.com

ISBN: 978-1-954116-12-2

Printed in the United States of America

Giving Thanks

I would like to give thanks to many people for the creation and publishing of this book.

I would like to give honor to Jesus Christ, my Savior and King, for giving me the words to write.

He has blessed me with the Trinity Outreach Program and its leaders: Master Shanae Dees, Pastor Seth Taylor, Master Sophia Taylor, Master David Hardin, Bishop Corlis Dees, Master Toby Lingg, Matt Ping, and Master Jenny Hardin.

Jesus has placed us at many Taekwondo tournaments throughout the state of Indiana. This is where we met Grandmaster Daniel Coblentz.

At one Taekwondo tournament in Greensburg, Indiana, Grandmaster Coblentz delivered a motivating speech about the USA flag. It was in that moment that I felt led by the Holy Spirit, first to take notes, and then to compose a poem in three days.

Thank you, Grandmaster Coblentz, for your faith in Jesus Christ; and thank You, Jesus Christ, for allowing my steps to cross paths with Grandmaster Coblentz, Tracy Winters, and all of the aforementioned people.

~ Dain Taylor

Foreword

What does the United States Flag stand for? I would like to know. It has red and white stripes that happen to give it a glow.

Twenty-six years of education should allow me to explain the reason why—for this flag is decorated with three specific colors and hangs freely in the sky.

I did not attain this answer from all my years in school. It happened to be at a Taekwondo tournament where a Grandmaster offered me a different view.

Let's go ahead and reveal what he proclaimed that very day.

Let it be a blessing to you, your children, and your family always.

~ Dain Taylor

Brothers and sisters, it's time! It's time! I say, to remember what the American flag stands for today, tomorrow, and always.

For so many times we've pledged allegiance,
with right hands placed on our hearts,
while overlooking the symbols, the history,
and the flag's original start.

The fifty white stars that we see
ever so bright and clear,
represent the core beliefs that the
fifty states, by tradition,
should cling to and hold so dear.

Core beliefs, based and rooted on God's Word,
the Bible. Yes! This happens to be true!
Let's dive deep in uncovering the meaning of
the background color BLUE.

BLUE represents the first freedom that we citizens should boldly and courageously share, which is the freedom to worship when two or three happen to gather in prayer.

But recent years have seen a decline for this one important need and right.

So, let's continue spreading God's kingdom of love and fighting the good fight.

**For it is by the name of Jesus
that all sinners and captives are set free.**

Freedom! Freedom! Freedom!
What a concept that we should explore.
Let's look at the color RED, for it
deals with all the bloody wars.

The primary color RED,
as any indivdual can see,
represents the sacrifice past and present,
soldiers dying for both you and me.

The bloodshed, tears, and sacrifice of
many soldiers, families, and friends

help us know the depth of service
that we can barely and truly comprehend.

Our task is not finished;
let's not leave the WHITE behind.
For it happens to deal with
the souls of all humankind.

You see **WHITE** is the color that represents God and all purity,

but we were separated by Adam and Eve's sin, and thus, we were proclaimed guilty.

But this was not what God intended, when forming us in our mothers' wombs.

So, He sent His Son, Jesus, to die on the cross and be raised the third day from a tomb.

So, teenagers, children, adults, parents, sons, and daughters everywhere ...

Let us remember this TRUTH, in regard to how much we should care about this American Flag that hangs so proudly from the rooftops of so many buildings.

Let it be a SYMBOL of the GOSPEL, that we should be ready to ...

testify and to always bring it to peoples, nations, countries, and races from all walks of life.

Let us continue to celebrate this American Flag and let us be joined together as brothers and sisters in Christ.

About the Author

Dain Taylor, an author in Shelbyville, Indiana, has been told by many that he has a way with words. His unique writing style uplifts and reminds people of their purpose and value in God's kingdom. Readers can find his blog, updates, YouTube videos, and books on his author website: www.simplydain.com.

He is the author of *Nikki's World: the Dog Walk*; *What Would It Have Been Like?*; and *Divine Messages of Lobo and Blanco: Looking Back at Me*.